P is for Pumpkin

www.SlothDreamsBooks.com
www.SlothDreamsPublishing.com
www.SlothDreams.com

Published by Sloth Dreams Books & Publishing, LLC.
Sloth Dreams Children's Books
Pennsylvania, USA
www.SlothDreamsBooks.com

All Rights Reserved.
ISBN: 978-9-5436-9015-2

P is for Pumpkin
Written & Illustrated
by KeriAnne Jelinek

A
is for apple picking

B
is for bonfire

C
is for apple cider

D
is for donuts

is for equinox

F
is for fall

G
is for geese

H
is for harvest

I
is for Indian corn

J

is for Jack o' Lantern

K
is for knit sweaters

L
is for leaves

M
is for maple syrup

N
is for nature walk

O
is for October

P
is for pumpkins

Q
is for quilts

R

S
is for scarecrow

T
is for Trick-or-Treat

U
is for umbrella

U
is for vines

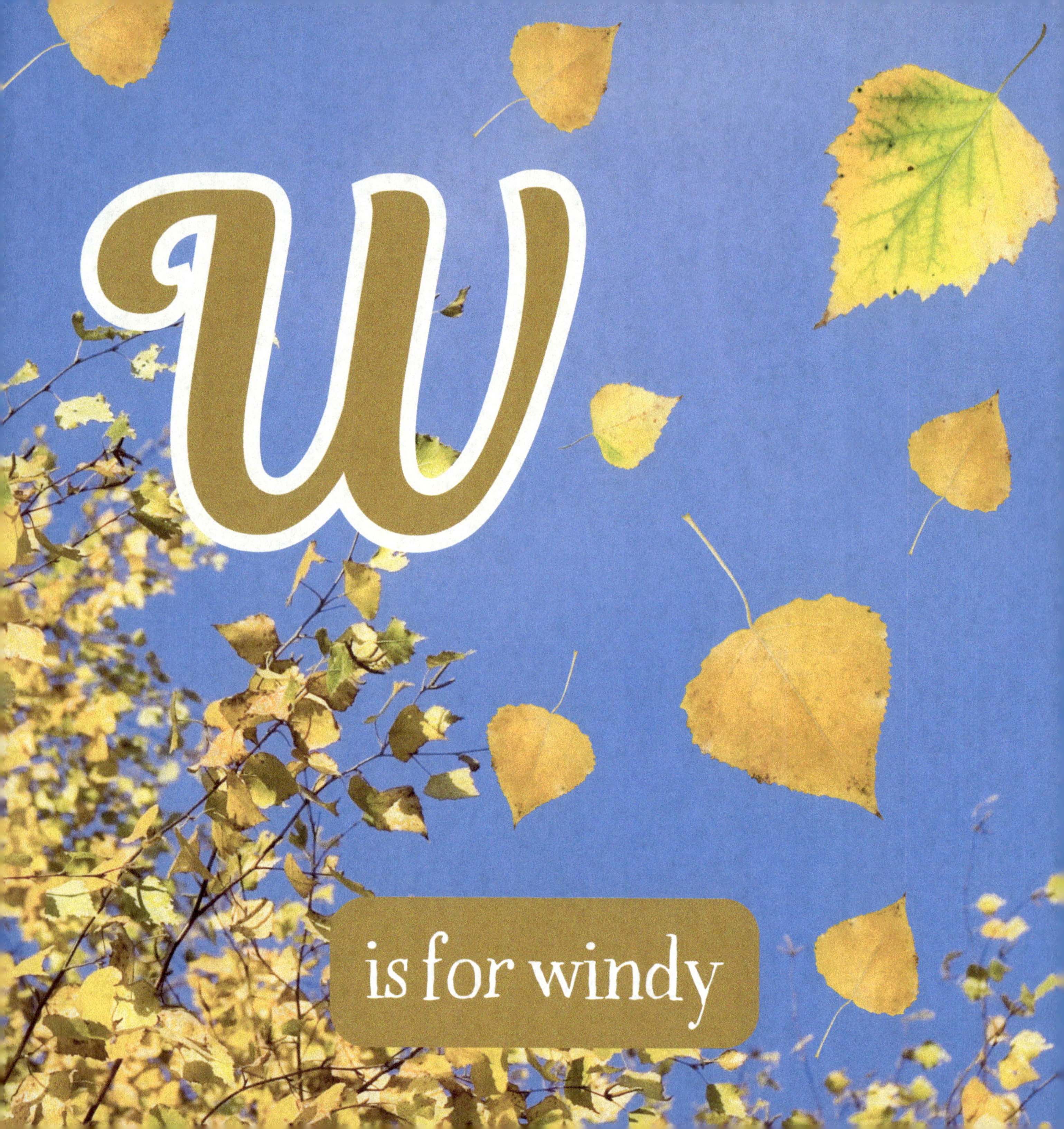

W
is for windy

X
is for eXtra layers

Y
is for yams

Z
CORN MAZE
is for corn maZe